Cell Phone Contract Breaker

Cell Phone Contract Breaker

Learn how to break your cell phone contract and move to better carrier

By: Larry Jacobs
ISBN-13: 978-1495203145

Cell Phone Contract Breaker

TABLE OF CONTENTS

Publishers Notes

Dedication

Unwanted CellPhone Contracts

Early Termination Fees

Surcharges vs. Non Surcharges

Get Rid of Your Carrier and Take Your Phone Number With You

How to Keep Your Cell Phone Number

Do You Need CellBreaker?

The Overall Process

Carriers Will Be Persistent

Now the Game Begins

Breaking your Contract Rightly or Wrongly

Know Your Contract and Watch for Changes

Winning Network Deficiency Claims

Deficiency Questionnaire

Cell Phone Contract Breaker

Calculate Your Savings

Breaker and Breaker Alerts

Order Process

About the Blog

ChitChatMobile Alternative

Select your service plan

Configure your features

Select the Phone

Accessories

See the Total

Signup

Ditch your Data Plan for WF-FI?

Promo Codes

Copyright

Disclaimer

Cell Phone Contract Breaker

PUBLISHERS NOTES

The procedure of getting out of an unwanted contract that you have with your carrier is fairly simple.

You need to carefully read the terms of your contract and then monitor the activities of your carrier, waiting for them to breach the terms of the contract.

When you discover the breach you then must object to the carrier about what actions breached the contract.

If the carrier then does not respond with an answer, you can then port your cell phone number to an alternate carrier. In effect, this then breaks the contact.

So as you can see, this is not very complicated thing to do. The problem is it does take some time.

And this is also not the end of the whole process. You know the carrier will claim that you own the early termination fee and they will go after you.

So this is where the chess match begins.

Cell Phone Contract Breaker

DEDICATION

This book is dedicated to my daughter, Demetra Gentry.

Unwanted CellPhone Contracts

Unwanted cellphone contracts are a big problem for many consumers. If a consumer wants out of a contact early, unfortunately they just don't have the right knowledge or experience to fight cell phone carriers successfully. If they do terminate the contract, they usually end up paying a big early termination fee.

What needs to be done in the industry?

1. The main thing is for cell phone carriers to stop making promises they don't keep.

2. Cell phone carriers need to get rid contracts and early termination fees.

CellBreaker.com is a company that was organized to help the cellphone consumer fight these carriers. They partners with consumers and is armed with the right knowledge and tools and in the end, it makes it less profitable for carriers to cheat their customers and lock them into sub-par cellphone service without any way to get out of them.

Read this book from cover to cover and then you will understand what you need to do to successfully get out of your cellphone contract legally without any early termination fees.

Cell Phone Contract Breaker

EARLY TERMINATION FEES

Did you know that according to an FCC report only 36 percent of cell phone consumers were familiar with their carrier bills and said that the bills included clear information about an early termination fee?

See FCC Report:

http://www.fcc.gov/encyclopedia/early-termination-fees

The problem is that most customers who knew about the termination fees did not know how much it would ultimately be.

If you dislike your cellphone service and want to get out of the contract, your main obstacle is the dreaded early termination fee.

To get out of the contract without a termination fee is to first find provider-side breaches and then demand a cancellation from the provider. It does take a lot of time and effort, but then in the end, you get out of the contract without the termination fee.

CellBreaker will help you get out of your carrier contact without an early termination fee. They have been extremely successful at this task.

SURCHARGES VS. NON SURCHARGES

This has nothing to do about getting out of your contract, but did you know about your carrier's charges.

What is the difference between surcharges and non-surcharges?

Non-surcharges include the itemized charges just pertaining to a service plan such as:

- Number of Minutes
- Amount of Data
- Usage Charges

Surcharges are the taxes, the government fees and other type of miscellaneous fees.

For more information how your carriers charges you with these go here:

Sprint customers

http://support.sprint.com/support/article/Know_about_Sprint_surcharges_taxes_fees_and_other_charges/case-ib376964-20090810-135914?docid=7561&docid=7549&navtypeid=6&pagetypeid=7&prevPageIndex=3&lid=y

Cell Phone Contract Breaker

Verizon customers

http://support.verizonwireless.com/support/bill.html

AT&T customers

http://www.att.com/esupport/article.jsp?sid=52264&cv=820#fbid=RcRML9Dj-Ct

T-Mobile customers

http://how-to.t-mobile.com/bill/

Get Rid of Your Carrier and Take Your Phone Number With You

Do you value your own cell phone number as much as I do? The possible threat of losing your phone number from switching to another carrier is very scary. So many customers stay with their carrier for the fear of losing the number in the process of switching.

It would be devastating for you to lose your cell phone number and very inconvenient to have to broadcast a new number to all of your friends and family.

Your cell phone number is pretty much like a piece of real estate. You could replace it but it would be very inconvenient.

No one wants to start from scratch with another cell phone number. There is no sense to it. Why should you have to lose your cellphone number just because you switched to a different carrier?

Learn how to keep your number in the next chapter.

Cell Phone Contract Breaker

How to Keep Your Cell Phone Number

If you follow the FCC guidelines you should be able to keep your cellphone number.

http://www.fcc.gov/guides/portability-keeping-your-phone-number-when-changing-service-providers

This is a summary of the guidelines:

1. If you want to take your cell phone number with you to a different carrier you must then ask your new carrier to pull your number from the old carrier and this is called a port request.

2. Do not terminate your old carrier account before you make that port request and it has been processed.

3. To send the port request to the old carrier, your new one does need your old account information. That will include:

- Your Name

- Your Account Number

- Your Address

- Your Phone Number

- Your Account Access Pin Number

Cell Phone Contract Breaker

It will normally take 1 business day to get the number moved over, but it can take as long as 7 days depending on if there are any problems. Once the port request is processed your contract with the old carrier will be effectively terminated.

Cell Phone Contract Breaker

Do You Need CellBreaker?

CellBreaker automates the process of getting out of your cell phone contract without any of the termination fees of the carrier. With CellBreaker's software you might spend 10 minutes throughout the entire process, whereas the carrier may spend 10-20 man hours just to keep up. At some point in time, the carrier will finally realize that it is not economical for them to continue to go after you for the termination fees and will finally give up.

CellBreaker is a nice product for putting the power into your hands to fight the cell phone carriers. Too frequently consumers like you are taken advantage by these carriers because you don't have the knowledge or time to fight. Without CellBreaker, you could easily spend twenty hours fighting with your carrier over a six-month period figuring how to get out of your contract.

CellBreaker will save you time and effort in figuring out how to get out of your cell phone carrier contract without pay early termination fees. They supply you with the tools that have been demonstrated to work successfully over and over again. They help you to identify what strategies work most effectively from others in your same situation. They take the pain out of you writing letters to your carrier and maintain the historical records for you.

There is nothing magical about this whole process. It does require continuous monitoring and a lot of attention to details and effective communication and persistence.

Cell Phone Contract Breaker

CellBreaker will help you stay on track and avoid the early termination fees and allow you to hold onto your phone number or numbers.

THE OVERALL PROCESS

To save you time and keep you focused, you need a partner to help you legally get out of your cell phone contract. Your partner is www.CellBreaker.com. The process is that neither you nor CellBreaker beach the contract to the carrier, but rather you wait for the carrier to make some change, but without your full permission. You then with the help of CellBreaker make a quick move to document the change and to acknowledge it.

Here are the three phases:

Detection:

1. Before CellBreaker can help you, they really need to know what is going on and why you don't want your cell phone account anymore.

2. Next they need to know the cell phones you need to cancel and the beginning and ending dates of service.

3. The name of the carrier.

With this information your partner, CellBreaker will monitor the carrier and then wait for them to, of course, break the contract agreement. This can be anything like just be changing fees, terms of service without your permission. Or it can be just poor quality service that you agreed on and paid for.

Cell Phone Contract Breaker

Objection:

When CellBreaker detects a change that they feel is actionable, they will put together a suitable communication to your cell phone carrier. It will document particulars of the change that they recognized. A reasonable about of time is then taken for the carrier to take delivery of the letter and correct the change. Then if no action is then taken by the carrier, you then can port your phone number to a preferred carrier from your problem carrier. After your phone number port is processed, your problem carrier will be unable to charge you for those numbers. This effectively then cancels your contracts with the old carrier.

End-Game:

Regrettably though, this does not really end the process as you probably figured. But it is the end of the customer affiliation with your old carrier. Normally your old carrier will then send the final bill that will, of course include the early termination fees. You are responsible for paying the legitimate charges, you are not, repeat not responsible for paying all of the early termination fees that the old carrier will levy against you.

CellBreaker has the information on your consumer rights and what strategies you need in dealing with your prior carrier.

Patience, persistence and using effective communication with the old carrier are the keys to success.

With that recipe, CellBreaker has a 100% success rate at eliminating the Early Termination Fees for their customers.

CARRIERS WILL BE PERSISTENT

Carriers don't want to give up the final early termination fee, so they will continue to assert that you owe it to them even though they forfeited it due to their own particular actions.

Say that you used CellBreaker to help you get out of your contract and you are very happy with your new carrier. If your old carrier sends you the early termination fee bill don't think you are alone, they do it to every customer that tries to get out a contract early.

Since carriers will do anything for lost revenue they will make false allegations to get as much money from you that they can. They will continue to send their bills hoping that you will eventually pay.

You don't need to have these carriers persecute you in this way. You have taken your first step now here is the next step to deal with the carrier's illegitimately alleged bills they send you.

First: Don't bother calling the carrier to complain. You are just wasting your precious time.

Second: You should only communicate with the carrier in writing. Your partner CellBreaker has a knowledge center full of pre-written, templates that are situation specific. You should use them. Just pre-populate them with your specific information and then print them out and mail them.

Third: Since you are right and the carrier is wrong, your goal is basically not to persuade your carrier that you are right, but to convince your carrier to cancel the alleged bills.

Fourth: To do this, then you must invoke some authority power over the carrier. I would recommend the State Attorney in your state. You can also use the Better Business Bureau, the Public Utility Commission, the FCC or the FTC. You can also invoke a number of consumer protection agencies. You do this by filing a formal complaint against the carrier.

You can use CellBreaker's archive of orders to state your case on each of the agency's electronic complaint form or addressing the agency's titled representatives. The agencies will force the carriers to either drop fighting you and responding to the formal inquiries and possible lawsuits from the agencies or just cancelling the bill they say you owe them. You have heard the saying that squeaky wheels are expensive to keep. So if you keep being squeaky, they will fold. It is not worth it to keep fighting you. They have a lot of others that they are fighting that are not prepared like you. So these others will probably give in and pay their alleged bills.

Fifth: So why do you need the power and authority of the agencies? The reason is simple, you yourself have no teeth. The carrier customer service representatives will not agree with you to waive the alleged bill. They have actually been trained to refute any such requests. Their primary goal is, of course, to retain you as a customer and diminish the lost revenue from you leaving their company. So you by contacting these protection agencies, you are presenting that

Cell Phone Contract Breaker

you know what you are talking about and are showing teeth that these carriers will fear. So you do need these agencies behind you.

Cell Phone Contract Breaker

NOW THE GAME BEGINS

Breaking your cell phone contract is pretty much like playing a chess game with an opponent. You need a strategy just like in chess. You execute your strategy one step at a time. As in chess your next move is up to what your opponent does. You really can't predict what your opponent will do. If you stick to your predefined rules you can't lose on a technicality. If your opponent makes a strategic error you can recognize it and then exploit it to your full advantage. Then you will have a victory.

Now on details of this game, your carrier is not very likely just to respond to your first objection with an OK, and say you are right and we give up. The carrier is more likely to come back with a NO objection. But this is just merely a procedural step that they do with everyone in this circumstance and it keeps you in a compliance with their set rules. You must understand the big picture here. Each and every step you do which is well documented authenticates our compliance with their rules and their final obligation to let you free without any fees. A documented case usually only takes three steps by sometimes it might take four or five depending on the carrier's ethics.

Carriers are famous for bullying individuals because that's what they do. They have more resources than you go and it's their job to get more money out of you. It's simply the classical bully on the playground and CellBreaker has learned how to deal with him. They have 100% success with these bullies and they don't give up until the carrier finally relents. They move fast and they move effectively.

Carriers basically employ two different tactics against their customers who attempt to affirm their rights. Cognitive dissonance and stalling is their primary tactics.

Stalling – This is where the carrier will stall and basically waste your time. They know that at some point you will just give up because you don't want to waste any more time. Where the carrier has unlimited time as this is their job to get money out of you. The carrier will just pass you from one agent to another and to different departments and it never ends. So you will give up because it is so time-prohibitive.

Cognitive Dissonance – This is where they will try to convince you that you are wrong by refuting each and every point that you make. They will do this by counter-positions that are not stated clearly. They will attempt to overload you with a bunch of nonsense which will make you doubt yourself and lose confidence in your position.

By using stalling and cognitive dissonance in their strategy against customers most finally give up, but not CellBreaker customers. CellBreaker is your partner in this fight and they don't let the carriers use these tactics against you and sucker you out of your money.

Carriers usually send early termination bills as soon as a customer cancels because they know that most will just pay it even though they probably don't owe it. Carriers know this and it makes good sense to them even though it is non ethical.

So you should keep two things in mind about this. CellBreaker customers don't fall into this trap because they know their legal rights and second, they know that if they follow all the rules and have a documented case that they are right and will win the situation and the carrier will lose.

Remember that on your side you have allies such as consumer protection, watchdog agencies and the government, all of whom have a job to protect your rights and keep the carriers honest. You can engage these allies any time but most of the time you don't have to.

Breaking your Contract Rightly or Wrongly

It is constantly in the news that carriers breach their contracts. And it is the notion by many that a breached contract can be broken. There are many articles out on the internet written by many authors concerning this.

You wonder if any of these authors of these many articles have actually broken a contract. None of the articles seem to give specifics of how to do it. It is really in the secret sauce that none of these authors talk about. They never really give the secret sauce level type details. So what that really means to me is that the authors really don't know how to do it or they don't grasp the details if they have done it and really broke a contract. There is not any one article that I could find that gives exactly the details precisely how to do it. The consequence of doing it incorrectly is that a person may actually lose the rights to a phone number, which they have had for a long time and have a lot invested in that number.

How do you know that the author of one of these articles knows what he is talking about? The best way is to ask yourself, do these plans address your objectives such as keeping your phone number and eliminating the early termination fees?

If you can get a yes then, of course you can proceed, but with high caution. Would you have bought a piece of real-estate based on reading a couple of sentences in an online article? Then you probably should not do that with your cell phone either.

You may not know that cell phone carriers are experts in disrupting well-informed and seemingly confident customers from their undertaking to affirm their contractual rights. Carriers are experts and they do this each and every day. This is their job. They have been doing this for years. They are experts in knowing how to trip their customers and how to stop them dead in their tracks. As I said above they are experts in using two tactics which are stalling you and cognitive dissonance.

First, let me explain their stalling tactic. Say your concern is for a $100 early termination fee. The carriers know that they can run out the clock on your patience and time and at some point you'll say to yourself, I can't spend anymore time at this. Do you want to spend time with arguments with agent after agent and even supervisors with messages and phone calls? It might take you 10 hours of your precious time. At say $10 per hour is it really worth it even if you are successful. Is it a really good use of your time? This is why most people don't follow their legitimate claims against these carriers. It is not good use of their time.

Second, consider their cognitive dissonance tactic. So say that you have good understanding of your rights of the contract and you know your rights were impinged upon. So say you have a winnable position in the beginning. Now you engage the carrier. You spent 10 hours in the arguments and conversations with agents. The conversations go something like this:

1) You state your situation position.

2) The carrier tells you how you're wrong.

3) You then insist that you're right.

4) The carrier then insists you are wrong.

This lengthy and infantile exchange leaves you doubting the soundness of your position. It's like the interrogation that induces confession of a man that is innocent. At some point you can't bear the noise anymore and you become doubtful of your rightness of your position and then you just give up.

There are not any articles out on the internet that talks about the real tactics used by these carriers.

The biggest point to all of this is there is a definite right way and a wrong way to break a contact with a carrier. Before you start the mission you need a sound plan and you must fully understand all the elements and what is at stake. Don't listen to the authors out on the internet that are ill-advised and naïve and don't know what they are talking about. What they propose in their articles is called cell breaking wrongly. You as a consumer who needs to break a contract with a carrier need to lean on the advice of an expert like CellBreaker who has successfully broken a large number of contracts. That is what you call cell breaking rightly.

KNOW YOUR CONTRACT AND WATCH FOR CHANGES

So when you walk into a carrier's store you peruse the store's selection of phones and talk to a sales person regarding the various plans.

You then pick out a phone, pay for it, then sign the receipt and leave with your new cell phone.

Did you know that your signature on that receipt is an agreement that you agreed to pay for the cell phone for 2 years? If you are like me that two-year commitment does not thrill you. You realize that if for some reason you needed to get out of the contract your carrier is going to zap you with a high early termination fee based on the contract terms.

But did you know that even before the ink dries on the receipt your carrier is going to change the contract terms?

They will notify you of the contract change in a small 8 pt. font notice hidden in a twenty page cell phone statement. If you are a detailed data person and read everything in the statement, you might notice it. But 99% of customers don't notice it. And even if you did notice it you probably won't know what it means.

Here is an example of what Sprint did when they issued a notice on their September 2013 statements:

Cell Phone Contract Breaker

GPS Navigation Removal from Data Plans
On 10/1/13, GPS services, Sprint Navigation and Telenav GPS Navigator, will be removed from bundled data and data add-on plans. For info on GPS Navigation alternatives (varies by device), visit sprint.com/navsupport. For Svc. Agreement info, see My Sprint or sprint.com/termsandconditions.

Customers who saw the change did not know what that meant to them. This was a vague disclosure with no press release. So if you did not notice it on your statement, you did not know that you experienced a loss of navigation without any notice.

You can reach out to the Sprint's forum on this:

https://community.sprint.com/baw/thread/129657

You will see that the Sprint's Social Care Team responded with the statement that Sprint's two competitors did not offer a GPS turn-by-turn application either.

Most people did not care about the competition, but to the fact that they signed a two year contract which included the GPS feature and now they would have to pay $9.99 per month to get it from here on out.

So you are still bound to the contract of your carrier unless you object to them for a contract change. Of course, the carriers don't want you to object to any change they do. They make it extremely difficult for you to notice any changes they make and what the changes mean to you. So they write their contracts that define exactly how and when you must object and well as the type of changes that they will allow you to object to.

Carriers do handicap you and they do this by withholding accurately and timely explanations of what any changes mean to you. If you are persistent and try to squeeze it out of the carrier, they will claim that the change is not unfavorable or materially important to you.

A contract is adversarial by nature. What that means is that for a contract to be valid both of the parties must of course give up something.

Unfortunately when a carrier changes a contract with you, it is almost always in the favor of the carrier and it is at your expense. The contract actually allows the carrier to make changes whenever it wants at the interest of you. You then have very little recourse in the wake of the alteration.

The carriers use "materially adverse" as the term of the change they made. You have no recourse but to either leave the contract after the change is made if it is, of course, measurable and adverse to you. The overall problem with this is that nowhere in the contract is the threshold defined.

Did you know that on July 1, 2013 Sprint made some very drastic changes to their contract for maximum duration of a call? If the call was too long they could terminate the call. Apparently Sprint feared that customers were abusing call lengths, especially those using their

Cell Phone Contract Breaker

cell phones as baby monitors. Customers worried that Sprint would terminate their calls exceeding some mysterious length. But their worry was definitely legitimate and CellBreaker helped a lot a Sprint Customers break their contract.

Winning Network Deficiency Claims

Did you know that the cell phone is an advanced and highly complicated technological piece of equipment? The reasons are:

- Because the many different engineering disciplines involved: Electrical, Mechanical, Radio Frequency, Software, etc.
- The design complexity
- The system has evolved through multiple generations—with each generation still functioning.

Given the above it is quite amazing that the cell phones work as good as they do! But this is the problem and that is really why carriers can't guarantee their performance.

Whenever you sell a complicated service like this and consider the consumer expense of it, there is an implied level of service to be expected by the consumer. The problem is there is no real way to define that level. But this situation does not give a carrier the right to take your money and not give you the service you paid for.

Is there a threshold on the number of dropped calls by a carrier? No. Carriers use this to their advantage. You need to capture hard data that can demonstrate that your expectation of service is not being met.

Cell Phone Contract Breaker

Carriers will throttle your date if you use too much over some abstract amount. If you use two units of data and others in the system use only one unit, then you are a candidate for throttling.

Cell Phone Contract Breaker

DEFICIENCY QUESTIONNAIRE

The following questionnaire analysis tool will help you to strengthen your position to break up with your carrier.

A. How many calls do you make per month looking at your last 3 statements?

B. Without a lot of solid information it is very difficult to build a solid case for you. These questions will help to solidify your case. (There are three failure types)

>a) How many times per month you could not make a call or make a data connection?

>b) How many times per month did you have a call dropped prematurely?

>c) Home many times per month was your quality of call was so poor you could not communicate effectively.

Compare your actual number of calls to your failure estimates. If the proportions are starting, then you need to start collecting actual hard data. Think in terms of going to court and trying to build a case where you are proving that you are not getting the service of what a normal person would expect. Failures are normal. You are using data to show the amount of failures you are experiencing is significantly beyond normal.

Cell Phone Contract Breaker

You need to record every time when you use your phone and had a problem.

1. Record the date and time of the problem.

2. Give a description of the problem. For example

    a) Call Fail

    b) Dropped Call

    c) Network Congestion

    d) No Service

    e) Poor Voice Quality

3. Where was the location of the problem? Give the street address, intersection or even a GPS coordinate.

4. Is the location of the problem a place to frequently visit?

5. When you had the problem were you outdoors or indoors? If it was indoors then where were you in the building? Give the floor or the exact location.

Cell Phone Contract Breaker

CALCULATE YOUR SAVINGS

Want to know how much you will save by breaking your cell phone contract now? Then go to http://cellbreaker.com/ and you'll find the page below. You can put your carrier's name in, the number of lines, contract length in months, months remaining.

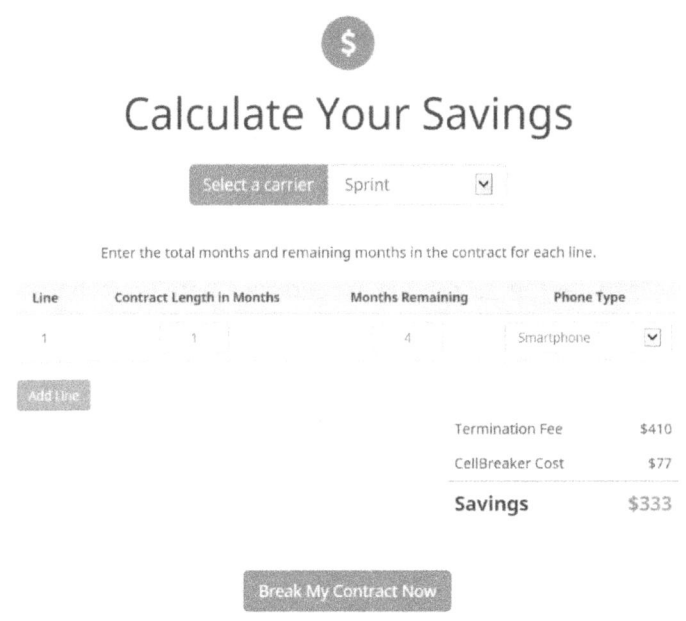

Cell Phone Contract Breaker

BREAKER AND BREAKER ALERTS

If you are now ready to break your cellphone contract you can start by using two different ways using CellBreaker.

One way you can order the service called "Breaker". It will save you a lot of time, money and all the frustration. They will help you realize when there are material changes with the carrier. Then they will automate the cancellation process for you and comply with your carrier's terms of service.

CellBreaker provides you with a 100% money-back guarantee to get you out of your cell phone contract without paying early termination fees.

The other was is to get the "Break Alerts" service. There is no charge for this. That way you will stay informed by CellBreaker monitoring your service. They will email you alerts of any material changes. There is no obligation to pay for this and they opinion and information you will get is free.

In interested then go here: http://cellbreaker.com/pricing

Cell Phone Contract Breaker

 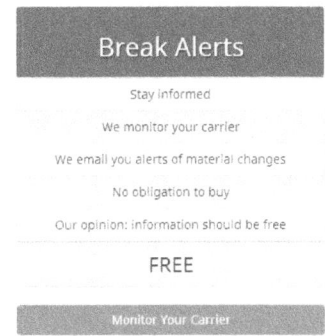

ORDER PROCESS

Then if you click the tab at the bottom Breaker, it will take you to the next page, which is a signup form.

Next put your email address in as well as a password you decide on.

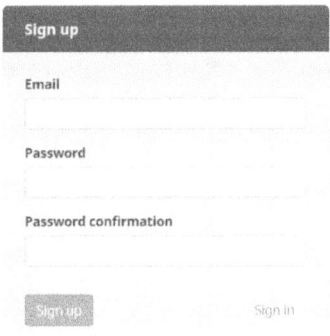

It will then take you to the next form. See next page.

Cell Phone Contract Breaker

Now put in your information as requested such as your account carrier and lines to break.

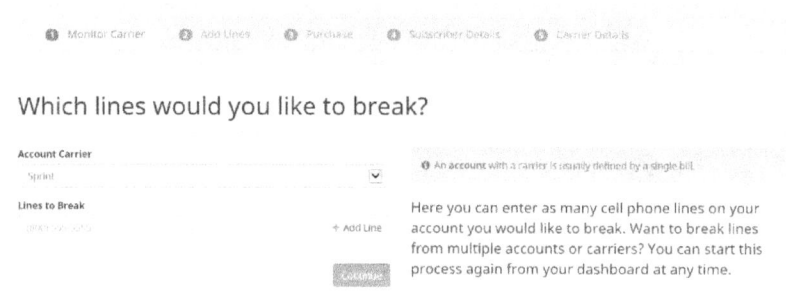

Cell Phone Contract Breaker

Then you can put in your credit card, expiration, security code and promotional code and place the order.

Readers of this book get a $5 discount with CellBraker.

To get your promotion code register at:
www.chitchatmobileforless.com

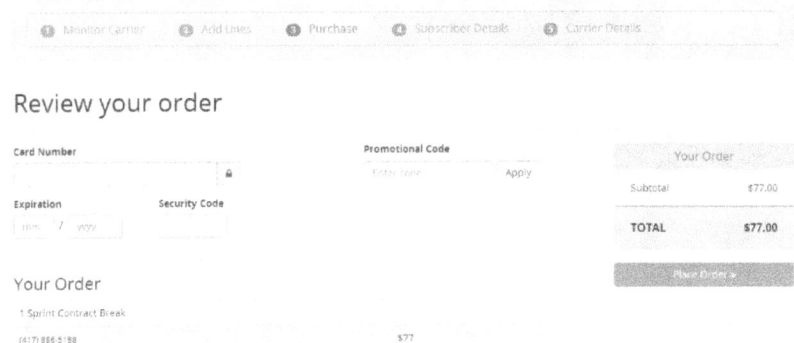

ABOUT THE BLOG

http://youtu.be/OHG93Y6kSvQ

The CellBreaker has a blog that is for basically two types of people.

http://blog.cellbreaker.com/

1) Disgruntled customers who are looking for some solutions to their cell phone problems.

2) People who already have hired CellBreaker to break their cell phone contract.

They call it *"The Breakery"* as it is designed to give a comprehensive treatment of the principles of cell phone customer provider relationships and an analysis of the most seen types of consumer complaints, poor customer service, unilateral changes and discussion of the necessary skills of cell phone contract breaking. It does reference to CellBreaker's Knowledge Center only accessible to CellBreaker's Customers. The blog is intended to present the principals of cell phone customer-provider relationship original posts. It applies these principals to particular types of cell phone problems in later posts.

Cell Phone Contract Breaker

CHITCHATMOBILE ALTERNATIVE

So when you eventually get out of your contract for various reasons such as the service was too expensive or it had poor service or whatever, you might want to consider a cellphone carrier that is high quality, inexpensive and is without a contract.

There are some out there that are excellent. One is www.chitchatmobile.com

With ChitchatMobile you get high quality service with no contract, no credit check. Their service works through a nationwide service. You can use your existing phone if it is compatible or buy a phone from them.

Their basic voice service starts at only $9.99 plus tax per month with unlimited text and free WI-FI!

So go to the next page to see how easy it is to sign up with them.

Cell Phone Contract Breaker

SELECT YOUR SERVICE PLAN

First select your service plan.

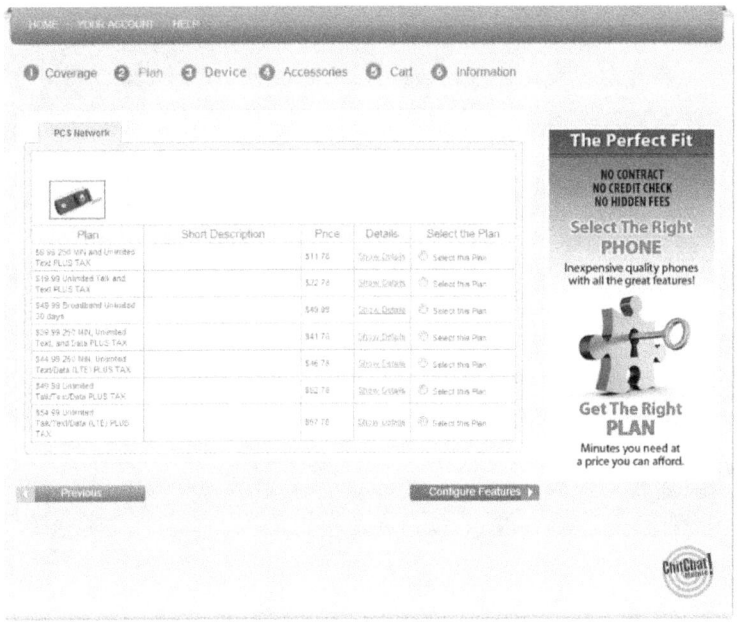

Go to the next page to configure the features.

43

Cell Phone Contract Breaker

CONFIGURE YOUR FEATURES

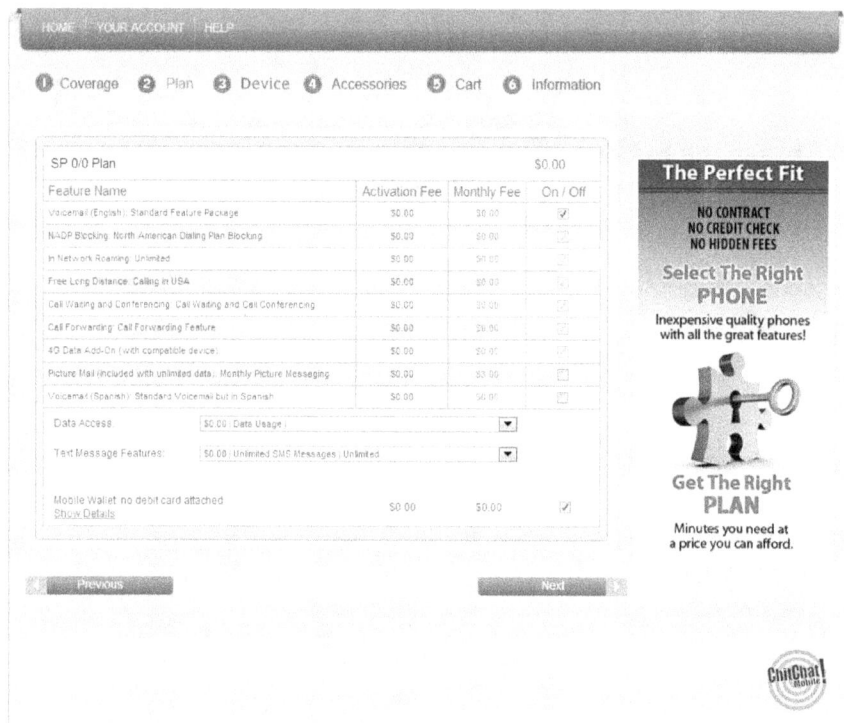

Go to the next page to select the phone or use your existing phone.

Cell Phone Contract Breaker

SELECT THE PHONE

If you already have a phone from your prior (Sprint compatible carrier) you can use it, or you can purchase new phone directly on the site.

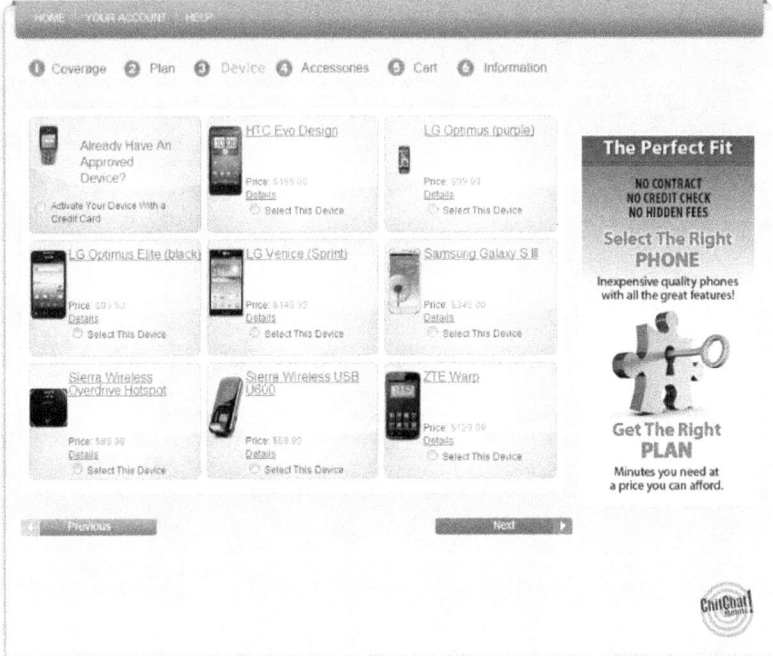

Go to the next page for accessories such adding minutes and data cards.

Cell Phone Contract Breaker

ACCESSORIES

Next select accessories such as cash cards for minutes or data:

Go to the next page to see the total.

Cell Phone Contract Breaker

SEE THE TOTAL

Go to the next page to see the final signup page.

Cell Phone Contract Breaker

SIGNUP

Be sure to put all the information in correctly and the cellphone numbers you want to port.

Readers of this book get free activation with www.chitchatmobile.com

To get your promotion code register at: www.chitchatmobileforless.com

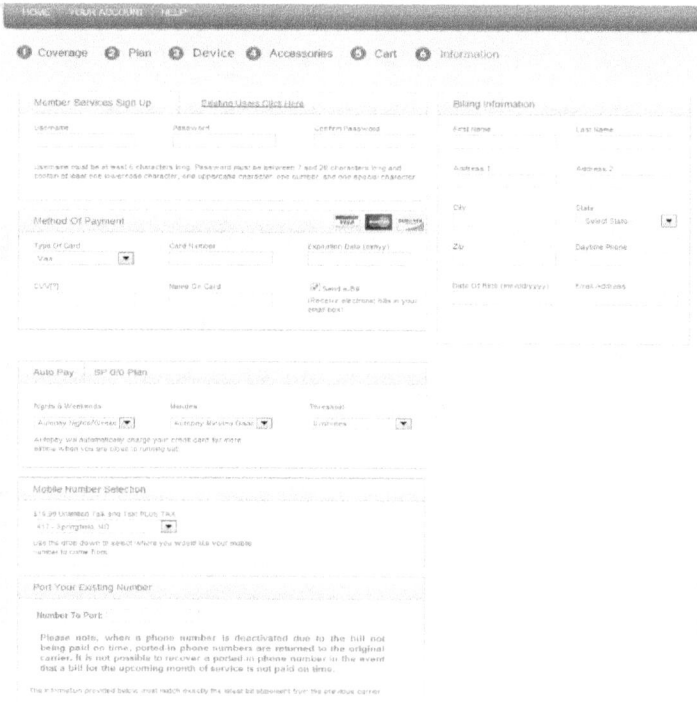

Cell Phone Contract Breaker

Next go this page and press the complete button to finish. It's just that easy. This will give you excellent cell phone service (voice, unlimited text and free WI-FI) at inexpensive prices.

Cell Phone Contract Breaker

DITCH YOUR DATA PLAN FOR WI-FI?

With all of the free WI-FI around, wouldn't it be great if your cell phone carrier allowed you to chuck your data plan and then you could just use free WI-FI to access the internet? Why should you still have to pay for expensive 3G and 4G wireless services? Since just about every smartphone comes with Wi-Fi built in, why can't you just subscribe to a voice/text service and use free Wi-Fi on your phone to access the internet instead of using the overpriced data plans available?

The problem is that most of the major cellphone carriers don't allow you to use a smartphone and have only a basic voice/text plan and use free WI-FI access the internet. The reason is that carriers make most of their profits from data plans and not on voice/text plans.

If you are willing to ditch the major carriers, you could try a new cellphone service from ChitChatMobile.com, which begins at $9.99 a month for talk plus unlimited text and WI-FI. ChitChatMobile buys and resells their service from the Sprint Nextel network. Using one of their smartphones you can use WI-FI for most of your data needs and if you need just some data on the go (where no WI-FI is not available) use their smaller data plans of 100MB for $5, 250MB for $10, 600MB for $20, 1000MB for $30, 1600MB for $40 or 2500MB for $50. They also have an inexpensive unlimited, talk/text/data plan for only $49.99 per month. See previous chapter.

Go to www.chitchatmobile.com

Promo Codes

As a reader of this book you can use our promo codes to get discounts with www.cellbreaker.com and www.chitchatmobile.com

$5.00 Discount with CellBreaker

Free activation with ChitChatMobile.com

To get these promo codes please go to our site:

www.chitchatmobileforless.com

Then register. By registering with us we can then keep you up with any changes that will affect you regarding breaking your contract with your carrier.

Cell Phone Contract Breaker

COPYRIGHT

Copyright 2014, Halliker's, Inc. All rights reserved. Information in this publication must not be reproduced in any form without written permission from the publisher.

DISCLAIMER

This book is for the general purpose of legally getting out of your cellphone contract when you are having problems with your service and or want to switch to a different carrier for any reason. The writer therefore does not assume any responsibility for liability or losses that might possibly occur as a result of this project that you might have chosen to undertake. You should always consult a professional person or company about this project. The writer of this book therefore does not assume any responsibilities for any errors, omissions or inaccuracies in this book.

www.ingramcontent.com/pod-product-compliance
Lightning Source LLC
Chambersburg PA
CBHW071824170526
45167CB00003B/1405